PARABLES AND PORTRAITS

PARABLES
AND
PORTRAITS

Stephen Mitchell

1817

HARPER & ROW, PUBLISHERS

New York

Grand Rapids, Philadelphia, St. Louis, San Francisco

London, Singapore, Sydney, Tokyo, Toronto

ACKNOWLEDGMENTS *Encounter*: "Job." *The Nation*: "Tao-chi." *The New Yorker*: "Jerome," "Spinoza." *Tikkun*: "Cinderella," "Achilles and the Tortoise," "Cherry Plums," "Hitler in Sheol," "In the Garden," "Faust," "Through the Eye of the Needle," "Left Hand," "Brief Theodicy," "Jonah," "Kingdom of Heaven." *Wigwag*: "Brooms." *Zyzzyva*: "The Frog Prince," "Huang-po," "At the Top of the Christmas Tree," "Cassandra," "Sinai." "Dr. Johnson," "Jerome," "Huang-po," "Kafka," "The Baal Shem Tov," "Tao-chi," "Spinoza," "Meister Eckhart," "Francis," "Picasso," "Montaigne," and "Vermeer" have been published as *Twelve Portraits*, in an edition of ninety-five copies, by Wesley B. Tanner at the Arif Press, Berkeley.

FIRST EDITION

Designer: David Bullen
Compositor: Wilsted & Taylor

LIBRARY OF CONGRESS CATALOG CARD NUMBER 89-45690
ISBN 0-06-016269-4

90 91 92 93 94   RRD   10 9 8 7 6 5 4 3 2 1

To Christie McDonald

CONTENTS

PARABLES
AND
PORTRAITS

CINDERELLA

Cinderella, the soul, sits among the ashes. She is depressed, as usual. Look at her: dressed in rags, face smeared with grime, oily hair, barefoot. How will anyone ever see her for who she is? A sad state of affairs.

Winter afternoons, in a corner of the kitchen, she has long conversations with her fairy godmother, over a cup of tea. The fairy godmother has, accidentally on purpose, misplaced her magic wand. In any case, these transformations are only temporary. The beautiful spangled gown, the crystal slippers, the coach and footmen—all would have disappeared at the stroke of midnight. And then what?

It is like the man in the mirror, says the fairy godmother. No one can pull him out but himself.

Ready, set at their respective starting places, staring into the distance between the parallel white lines, they seem like an old married couple about to run through the same argument for the millionth time. Achilles is tense inside his huge golden muscles. The tortoise blinks.

Afterward, they shower; then walk, side by side, to a neighborhood café.

"It's the damnedest thing," says Achilles. "The more I catch up, the more reality slows down. Until it's no longer even a film. Every time: we finish, immobilized, in a single frame."

"With me a micro-meter ahead," the tortoise adds, sighing. He takes another bite of his lettuce sandwich; chews for a while, meditatively; blinks.

"Maybe if I tried something different," Achilles says. "Maybe a new pair of shoes."

CHERRY PLUMS

They grow all over Berkeley, along the sidewalks, and start to ripen in May. They are tart but delicious. We stop on our after-dinner walk, reach up and pluck a few. Or fill our pockets from the trees in the empty lot across Vine Street. She bites into the first one as I watch. "Mmmm," she says, "plum cherries."

"No no, sweetheart. Cherry plums."

"Oh you. I've *always* called them plum cherries. They *look* like cherries."

"But they're plums. They taste like plums. They're called cherry plums because they're so small."

"Well I don't care. *I* call them plum cherries."

The title of this parable is "Plum Cherries."

I needed to write a parable about Hitler. My friend said "Don't."

I sat down at my desk and waited. What I glimpsed was an afterworld. There were no physical torments. Only this: that he had to relive his life, as actor and observer both, a thousand times, out to the farthest consequence of his acts, with a constantly growing awareness of the horror, and a constantly growing, unbearable, shame. (In that world there are no ideas to escape into.)

I showed the parable to my friend. He winced. He said, "You have no right to imagine it that way."

I said, "But according to our sages, on the last day even Lucifer will be forgiven."

He said, "You must crawl to the very center of evil before you can see the stars."

DR. JOHNSON

Something I left behind
calls me back to your time-zone,
when the son of man spoke Latin,
tucked lace in his collar, and upon
his brachycephalic dome
an equilateral velvet
hat was perched, like a dove.
Through the great marble hallways
of the British Museum, the ghost
of Descartes wandered, bemused.

If I were to find you now,
it could not be in the light.
You would have no chandeliers blazing,
no circle of friends around you
as, steadily, immensely, you poured
the distillates of your Tory
wisdom into their ears.
What, Sir, remains when the body,
one-eyed and scrofulous,
which lurched through the streets as in fetters
and rode horses like a balloon—
what remains when that body
casts off its cumbrous frame?
When all the splendid distinctions,
the intricate structures of right
and wrong, the golden yardsticks,
the algebras of dismay
vanish, you are left alone
with the sense of infinite vastness

that a child awakens to, blissful
or terrified, in the dead of night.

Perhaps you're prepared to stay there.

Or perhaps, out of the fond
and unassuaged depths of your spirit,
an image, like a flower blooming
in fast motion, begins to form,
the vision of a shapely leg,
the sweet cavern between two thighs.
And soon it is, yes, a world:
of consonants pullulating
and innocent flute-voiced vowels;
soon there are nests of quartos,
folios flap through the air
like homing geese, and the towers
and bridges of a city loom up
in the gray foreground. Those crowds—
are they heading into the Strand?
Those gentlemen in wigs and waistcoats—
are they bound for The Cheshire Cheese?

All right, Sir: let us begin
again. You are in the courtyard
of some country alehouse, fidgeting
in a coach of white and gold.
The driver (can you see?) is a dachshund.
The team are four brown mice.
Don't be impatient. Take out
your handkerchief. Blow your nose.
We'll be leaving in a moment. London
is no farther off than a sigh.

MANJUSHRI

My wife and my old Zen Master both were born at the cusp of July and August; so I know something about lions. It takes a while to get used to their habits. But once you have let them eat you alive, once they have picked you clean and left nothing but your white bones gleaming in the sunlight, you will find that you are perfectly at ease.

Take this figure of Manjushri, Bodhisattva of wisdom, Buddha before the fact. The lion he is enthroned upon looks like one of those huge good-natured dogs that will let a child pull its whiskers, or almost twist off its ears, without complaining. Chin resting on its paws, tail tucked neatly under its belly, it is imperturbable, because it knows who is the boss.

Manjushri himself sits, formal but relaxed, in a semi-lotus position, with one leg dangling over the lion's right flank. Both his hands are clasped around the sword of spiritual discernment (one edge kills, the other gives life). He holds the sword straight up, invitingly, with a little grin.

"Living Buddhas are a dime a dozen," the lion thinks, "but a good wooden Buddha is hard to find."

Eve bites into the fruit. Suddenly she realizes that she is naked. She begins to cry.

The kindly serpent picks up a handkerchief, gives it to her. "It's all right," he says. "The first moment is always the hardest."

"But I thought knowledge would be so wonderful," Eve says, sniffling.

"Knowledge?!" laughs the serpent. "This fruit is from the Tree of *Life*."

LAZARUS

He had almost reached the end of the tunnel when he heard his friend's voice calling him back. The voice was filled with love, but also with sorrow and pity, and not so much fear of death as resistance to it, as if it were an enemy to be expelled or overcome. He had realized so much, during the four days' journey, that these resonances struck him as odd, coming as they did from a man of such insight; struck him as laughable, as almost childish. All the dramas of his short, intense life were an instant away from being resolved, dissolved, in the light at the end of the tunnel, which was not a physical light—after all, he no longer had physical eyes—but a radiant presence, a sense of completion a million times more blissful than what he had felt even in the company of his beloved friend. And the sweet, seductive drama of master and disciple, how childish that had been too, as if a candle flame needed to warm itself before a fire. He thought of his sisters in the old house in Bethany, of Mary anointing their friend's feet and wiping it with her hair: the tenderness, the absurdity of that gesture.

The voice was still calling. He didn't have the heart to refuse. He knew that, for his friend's sake, he would have to postpone his disappearance, to hurry back down the tunnel and return to his body, left behind so gratefully, which had already begun to stink.

Greater love has no man.

FAUST

Faust begins by cutting into a circle. This, given the purity of his intent, eventually leads to mass pollution and fifty thousand nuclear warheads pointed at everything he loves.

He does not enter the world as the first Adam entered Eve. There are other ways of knowing.

JEROME

In Dürer's engraving
you sit hunched over your desk,
writing, with an extraneous
halo around your head.
You have everything you need: a mind
at ease with itself, and the generous
sunlight on pen, page, ink,
the few chairs, the vellum-bound books,
the skull on the windowsill that keeps you
honest (*memento mori*).
What you are concerned with
in your subtle craft is not simply
the life of language—to take
those boulder-like nouns of the Hebrew
text, those torrential verbs,
into your ear and remake them
in the hic-haec-hoc of your time—
but an innermost truth. For years
you listened when the Spirit was
the faintest breeze, not even the
breath of a sound. And wondered
how the word of God could be clasped
between the covers of a book.
Now, by the latticed window,
absorbed in your work,
the word becomes flesh, becomes sunlight
and leaf-mold, the smell of fresh bread
from the bakery down the lane,
the rumble of an ox-cart, the unconscious
ritual of a young woman
combing her hair, the bray
of a mule, an infant crying:

the whole vibrant life
of Bethlehem, outside your door.
None of it is an intrusion.
You are sitting in the magic circle
of yourself. In a corner, the small
watchdog is curled up, dreaming,
and beside it, on the threshold, the lion
dozes, with half-closed eyes.

THE FROG PRINCE

Gorgeous, charming, rich (and spiritually mature as well), the Prince lies musing on his firm but sensitive king-size mattress. He and the Princess have just finished making love. It was wonderful, as always. Now she is curled alongside him, facing away into her own dreams, knees drawn up, her sweet, slightly flat little ass cushioned by his belly and thighs. She is snoring, lightly—or would you call it an intense purr? It is music to his ears.

He lets his mind drift back to the days before the miraculous transformation. Yes, the Princess knew that their karma was interwoven like warp and woof, but this didn't prevent her from being furious. It was more than simple dislike: she was disgusted. And he had to admit, even then, that with his bulging eyes and clammy green skin and amateurishly patched-up heart he was not the world's most attractive bachelor. Still, he had some redeeming qualities. Such as? Well, determination, for one thing. He had hopped all the way from the muddy pond to the palace, up the white marble stairs, under the door, up the white spiral staircase to the Princess's bedroom. What an effort! And all the way that obnoxious sound: *squish, squush.*

His finest moment, though, had come when the Princess picked him up to hurl him against the wall. He could, after all, easily have slipped out of her impatient grasp. But he knew the stakes. It was now or never. And he trusted her aim.

BROOMS

Brooms make excellent dance partners. Though they are bald and armless, and have skinny, inflexible torsos, they more than compensate by their willingness to follow your lead. Draw them across the floor gently but with assurance. Remember to concentrate your willpower in your left hand. They will be completely at your disposal. They are courteous beings. If, occasionally, by mistake, they should happen to (ever so lightly) step on your toes, they will always apologize by simultaneously dusting off your shoe.

GREAT-GRANDFATHER CHANG

At last! An ancestor who understands.

It is 1910. He has taken off his identity as editor of the Shanghai *Times*, put on a spiffy new black silk *minàp* and a kind of squarish silk yarmulke, and gone down to the photographer's studio in search of a metaphor. He has no idea that in forty years his great-granddaughter will be born across the ocean or that in seventy-eight years his great-grandson-in-law will be staring, in huge admiration, at the faded trick photo, in which, both guest and host, he is seated benignly on a mahogany throne, and is also kneeling at his own feet, palms together in supplication. In case I didn't get the point, down the right side of the picture he has indulgently written, in nine finely brushed characters which I can't read: "Whatever you require, the only one who can give it is yourself." Both faces are smiling.

JOB

1

During the first stage of suffering, Job's companion was a worm
that had lodged itself in one of his open sores. Job would pass the
time brooding; the worm, exploring. Job would narrow his eyes
and try to see through the dark cloud-bank overhead. Or would
stare at the supple, slowly digesting worm as if it were a messenger
from another world.

Eventually, they came to know each other quite well.

2

Of course the friends were blond and clean-shaven and had no
trouble making their hexameters scan.

They reasoned thus: that although degradation was no proof
of viciousness, it did indicate bad judgment, or incompetence.
Item: Job's nose was irredeemably hooked. Item: Job's face was
crisscrossed by whole networks of unhappiness. His potential
vindication, they declared, had already begun to create havoc in
the realm of Nature. Birds fell, confused, from the blue sky; lions
lost their appetites; a large date-palm had been seen pacing in the
wilderness.

What did he expect, anyway? A medal?

3

Suddenly Job understands:
there is perfect
justice: not later.
Not later; but always now.

In that first moment of waking,
he sits up,
stunned, not recognizing even

himself, not needing to hear
the morning-stars burst out singing,
or the angels explode with joy.

4

"In any case," the friends said on their way home, "his offensive-
ness has not diminished. A miracle is no cure for bad breath."

HUANG-PO

Closer than we can know
and too true to be good, its image
flashes everywhere we turn.
Marvelous!—Tut, tut, it's nothing.

THROUGH THE EYE OF THE NEEDLE

The camel catches his breath, wipes the sweat from his brow. It was a tight squeeze, but he made it.

Lying back on the unbelievably lush grass, he remembers: all those years (how excruciating they were!) of fasting and one-pointed concentration, until finally he was thin enough: thaumaturgically thin, thread-thin, almost unrecognizable in his camelness: until the moment in front of the unblinking eye, when he put his front hooves together. Took one long last breath. Aimed. Dived.

The exception may prove the rule, but what proves the exception? "It is not that such things are possible," the camel thinks, smiling. "But such things are possible for *me*."

LEFT HAND

He is the awkward one, the fool, the younger brother. Can't manage sword or scissors. Bungles it when he tries to use a pen. He is good only for joint projects with his accomplished partner, and menial tasks, like lifting a cup or opening a book.

But he doesn't mind. He accepts his limitations, sees nothing sinister in the fact that grace is reserved for someone else. Perhaps that is why he has been chosen to wear the golden circle, promise of all fulfillment: the marriage ring.

Sometimes, after a day among the swine, he would be afraid to lie down in his wretched hut. Actually, the swine weren't bad company. They were intelligent animals, not any greedier than decent men he had known; he came to enjoy feeding them and hosing them down. They would close their eyes under the spray, grunt contentedly as the water washed away their grime and left them, if not whiter than snow, at least tolerably clean, then prance around in giddy pleasure, kicking up their heels.

The worst company was himself.

Sometimes he would be annoyed to a frenzy by a buzzing fly in a corner of the hut. He would stalk it from resting-place to resting-place; then, teeth clenched, he would dispatch it with a single stroke of his palm. If it had been merely stunned, he would impale it and set it on fire. He could feel his heart assuaged for an instant as the translucent wings went up in a flash and left, at the end of the pin, a tiny charred ball.

Many years later, after his own pain had been transformed in a different kind of fire, he made a vow never again to kill a fly. Whenever one of them trespassed into his house, he would trap it in a jar he kept under the sink (sometimes, with a hyperactive fly, this could take five or ten minutes). Then he would release it from a window or bring it outside to freedom. It wasn't out of guilt, or out of compassion, that he made this vow, since he saw quite clearly that he was responsible for everything in his life. But simply as a reminder: to acknowledge that once upon a time he had been stopped at the crossroads of the horrible and the sacred.

ISAIAH

The seraphim had been almost too polite. They had nodded, they had tsked, they had poured tea, they had moved their huge, iridescent dragonfly wings (each of them had six) as if in rhythm to his breathing. But they were obviously bored with his excuses, and would have been only too happy to get up from the table, say goodbye, and return to their fiery games. The one sitting next to him, whose face resembled his own, down to the minutest detail, though bliss made it appear in- or hyper-human, looked at him with a mixture of amusement, deep compassion, and disgust. It seemed to be exerting all its considerable spiritual force to suppress a laugh. Finally it rose, picked up something from the altar, and stood beside him looking in the direction of his lips. An unspoken question filled the air with dry heat, like a sauna.

Already he could smell his flesh burning.

FREUD

Your friend the Sphinx had promised you
the subtlest of all rewards
if someday you could solve her riddle.
Two-legged at noon, you remembered
the advice of another lady.
You knew that to know yourself
you would have to delve where the old ones
had already tapped,
and crawl where the small four-legged ones,
unaware of your problem,
blissfully sucked their toes.
It was a quest, of course.
The path began in the bedroom
and wound around and around
the back-lit kingdom of dreams.
But when you returned, with the taste
of knowledge bitter in your mouth,
there was no small hand to guide you
through that other darkness,
into the sacred grove.

A solemn story.

But suppose we begin again.
You are standing, new and ardent,
in front of the Sphinx. She has asked you
a question (your life depends on it)
that can barely fit into words.
Her eagle-winged, snake-tailed, lion's
body is comfortably poised
in the hot sand. Her face is lovely,
neither old nor young; at the corners
of her eyes are the wonderful sunburst

wrinkles when she smiles; her long
blue-black hair lightly
touches her naked breasts.
Careful . . . Careful . . . Think . . .
(though you will not solve it by thinking):
Who are you? Where do you come from?
Why do you feel afraid?

THE BINDING OF ISAAC

1

Abraham is caught in a dilemma. In parable, he must sacrifice his beloved son, even if a substitute should miraculously appear, bleating, within the thicket. In fact, however, the command is obviously demonic and he must refuse. In parable, he is a paragon of wisdom; but he is a homicidal maniac in fact.

It's as if someone were to reach out toward the face in the mirror and, with two-dimensional silvered-glass fingers, touched warm flesh.

2

As he grew up, Isaac remembered everything but the terror. He could still feel the weight of the firewood as he unstrapped it from the donkey's back, could still smell the crisp, pine-scented autumn air, could hear the two sets of footsteps crunching the pebbles on the trail up Mount Moriah. But not the final moment; he had long since forgotten that: the moment when he waited, trussed up on the altar, the carving knife quivering against his breast, his father's huge eyes above him, exalted and horrible. Over the years, as his own eyesight grew dim, the nightmare gradually acquired the details of a pious legend. The demented thought became a heavenly command. The distorted features became an expression of infinite fatherly concern. The abrupt awakening became a miraculous, last-minute reprieve from a God who was only testing, after all.

Whatever experiences we cannot bear to be conscious of, we must repeat in all their anguish. Thus Isaac grows blind. He is betrayed by his wife and younger son. He goes to the grave a disappointed, frightened old man, perhaps with blue numbers etched onto his right arm. It will take much hard work, many hundreds of rebirths, before he is ready to have the last laugh.

Of all human comestibles, the lemon is most nearly allied to the sun. Therefore we can deduce that the god of lemons is bright, slow-moving, and thorough. He delights in the primary, the elliptical. He is not overly concerned with sweetness.

Thus, lemon juice is the traditional cure for scurvy and optimism.

JONAH

After the first few hours he came to feel quite at ease inside the belly of the whale. He found himself a dry, mildly fluorescent corner near one of the ribs, and settled down there on some huge organ (it was springy as a waterbed). Everything—the warmth, the darkness, the odor of the sea—stirred in him memories of an earlier comfort. His mother's womb? Or was it even before that, at the beginning of the circle which death would, perhaps soon, complete? He had known of God's mercy, but he had never suspected God's sense of humor. With nothing to do now until the next installment, he leaned back against the rib and let his mind rock back and forth. And often, for hours on end, during which he would lose track of Ninevah and Tarshish, his mission, his plight, himself, resonating through the vault: the strange, gurgling, long-breathed-out, beautiful song.

KAFKA

Whoever has, even once, glimpsed
the certainty of our freedom
cannot be content with anything
less. He must sit in darkness
with his terrible yearning stuck
in his throat, unable to swallow,
unable to cough it out.

You, more than anyone, told
that most ancient of Jewish stories,
since it was your own. Exile
was the air you breathed, the water
you turned into living blood.
You saw that only one thing
is required of us: endless patience,
since the downward Way of despair
is not yet the way out, and the answer
must wander, bewildered, searching
for a question it will never find.

Sometimes you could feel in your words
an escape from the other voices.
What you heard yourself say, at night,
with nobody listening,
was a comfort—the *only* comfort:
that in eternity you were
an episode; a mere knot
of resistance to the dark love
that flowed all around you; a palimpsest
with the faint traces
of somebody else's writing.
Why should you want them saved,

those notes and stories that were just
the same old story? In the light
that was once too strong for your eyes,
you knew that they didn't matter.
They didn't matter in the least.

The first few were easy. The dog looked just like a "dog," the cat like a "cat," etc. He pointed to the cow, the horse, the wolf, the squirrel, and immediately the right word sprang into his mind. God stood beside him beaming, like a proud parent. (The only slight problem came after God wrote down "tiger" in his spiral notebook, and *he* kept, uncomfortably, feeling that it should have been spelled with a *y*.)

It wasn't until the pig trotted up to him from the line of patient animals who had not yet been named, that he had trouble. He wanted to say "pig," but the word stuck in his throat. Somewhere on the way to his palate it had run into a difficulty, he became aware of some discord that would have to find its resolution before he, or his descendants, could be complete. How much murky emotion, how many bad metaphors, lay hidden like seeds inside that name. A fascinating creature, though. All right. "Pig."

After this everything went smoothly. Aardvark. Bandicoot. Capybara. Pangolin. Gnu.

("Is that spelled N-u?" God asked.

"*G*-n-u.")

AT THE TOP OF THE CHRISTMAS TREE

Soon it will be dawn, and I wait up here with a heavy heart. I am shorter than the others. My hair isn't golden like theirs, but black and scratchy as steel wool. My wings look like wet fur. Even my gown needs pressing. It's hard to be a Jewish angel.

Years ago, when I arrived, new from the factory, the day before Christmas, I thought that my heart would burst. Imagine: to-morrow the Messiah would be born; the world would be trans-formed; no more suffering, good will toward men for ever and ever, as my heavenly colleagues had announced. But night came, and morning came, and it was the same old world. Every Christmas: it was the same old world.

So I wait here, out of my element it seems, with the tinsel, the lights, and all the other, happy, unthinking ornaments. My wings are folded behind me. A tear, permanent, hangs from the corner of my eye, like a tiny almond.

He tiptoes into the room almost as if he were an intruder. Then kneels, soundlessly. His white robe arranges itself. His breath slows. His muscles relax. The lily in his hand tilts gradually backward and comes to rest against his right shoulder.

She is sitting near the window, doing nothing, unaware of his presence. How beautiful she is. He gazes at her as a man might gaze at his beloved wife sleeping beside him, with all the concerns of the day gone and her face as pure and luminous as a child's and nothing now binding them together but the sound of her breathing.

Ah: wasn't there something he was supposed to say? He feels the whisper far back in his mind, like a mild breeze. Yes, yes, he will remember the message, in a little while. In a few more minutes. But not just now.

THE BAAL SHEM TOV

All the old metaphors
are speechless, and the old truths
lie on exhibit in the morgue,
each with an oaktag label
on its big toe. Unless I am there,
Gautama is still questioning
under the Bodhi tree,
while in Bethlehem Mary's womb stays
heavy, the ox and ass
looking on in mute compassion.

In the forest where you grew up
there was a small clearing
you liked to pray in. You would watch
the projects of the ants, or follow
a spider as it strung its web
in the crook of a maple-branch. Birdsong
unwound above you in lucid
confirmation. Whenever
you happened on the bloody remains
of a rabbit or squirrel, you buried them
gently, and recited
the Blessing upon meeting sorrow
face to Face. Prayer was
a quality of attention.
To make so much room
for the given
that it can appear as gift.

Years later they would come to you,
the doubters and the devout,
asking their pathless questions.
You wanted to get down on all fours.

You wanted to moo, or stand there
on tiptoe, flapping your wings.
What could you say, when the Good Name
was everywhere *you* were, uttered
by nightstorm and cloud and sunlight,
in fervor or grief. The few words
that you did find seemed
tinier than colored pebbles.
You had to pull them up quickly,
quickly, from far away.

PATIENCE

She used to show her guests an anchor, an hourglass, a key. That was in the days when symbols lived in an extended family and were racially homogeneous.

Now you must enter her house blindfolded. There is no furniture. No conversation. Oh, she will bring you a cup of water now and then, or a bowl of porridge, but always without a word.

If you are tempted to leave, remember the reports of those who have been here before you. How each one suddenly felt, after years or decades, the blindfold taken off by the softest of invisible hands, saw the bread and wine appear, and the candles in their crystal holders. And how, after the solitary meal, he was guided up the winding stairs to her bedroom. How the door opened by itself, and her soft, fragrant voice said, "Come in."

THE GOOD SAMARITAN ET AL.

The priest, the Levite, the Samaritan, and the man who fell among thieves meet in heaven to talk over old times. Since heaven has no past or future, they find themselves in the inn on the road to Jericho.

"I felt awful about not helping you," the priest says. "My heart wasn't open enough. But I'm working on it."

"The last time I had stopped to help a wounded man by the roadside," the Levite says, "he beat me and ran off with my wallet. I was afraid."

"It was my good fortune to be in the right place at the right time," the Samaritan says. "I didn't stop to think; the oil and wine poured themselves, the wound bound itself. My only problem came later, dealing with all the praise."

The man who fell among thieves takes another sip of wine. "Charity begins at home," he says. "If I had been kinder to myself, I wouldn't have been in that mess to begin with. But I am very grateful to all three of you. It takes great humility to step aside, for a parable's sake. And without the parable, I would never have been saved."

CELLO

It rests inside its close-fitting red-velvet-lined case the way medieval monks slept inside their coffins. But it doesn't meditate on death; it has already died, and barely remembers sunlight, water, the wind among the branches. It lies there in the dark, feeling all through its graceful curves the memory of a hundred years of music, and sometimes dreaming of heaven: the Bach suites.

Taken out to be played, it knows that by itself it is nothing, that it would be incapable of producing a single note even if it were a Stradivarius. So it gladly assents to having its strings tightened, painful though this is; it wants to be perfectly in tune, stretched to its utmost but not straining. When it feels ready, it leans back and waits for the bow to be drawn across, for the resonance to fill it completely.

TAO-CHI

Dressed in his long, white, long-sleeved,
blue-sashed holiday robe,
with a fashionably wispy beard
and some kind of Confucian doodad
on his head (it looks like a lantern),
the poet stands, face slightly tilted
upward, in the little grove.
It is just the first month of spring.
Yellow blossoms have appeared
on some of the branches. Others
are still bare. He is probably watching
the four or five black birds perched
on the central tree. Or perhaps
he is looking across to the left-hand
side of the page where, ending
a quote from Tu Fu, the character
for *human being* is inscribed
in two breathtakingly elegant
brush strokes. The ground is marshy.
A light wind rustles his robe.
Suddenly, with a shock, he realizes
that nothing in this life—nothing—
nothing—is ever lost.

PASCAL'S VISION

Weaned too fast and permitted to grow up among numbers, the mind frightens itself with false immensities. It creates mathematical time, uniform and uninterruptible; imagines mathematical space and floats off in the darkness between stars, a lost child. Bewildered by quantity, it has nightmares of multiplied pain— Armenians, Auschwitz (shhh)—and forgets what every child knows: that nothing is ever suffered in plural.

There is only one body. Only one death.

PINOCCHIO

Everything would have been fine if he had been an obedient puppet. Geppetto *said* that he wanted a real boy, but what he really wanted was someone made in his own image, someone to carry on his name: a chip off the old block. Of course, there was the matter of the periodically elongating nose. All of a sudden, before he even knew he was telling a lie, he would feel it itch; then, to his chagrin, it would pop out from his face, half-inch by half-inch, like the time-lapse photograph of a burgeoning plant. But with a little more self-awareness, he was sure, this obstacle too would eventually be resolved.

The real problem was that he had fallen in love; with a flesh-and-blood girl, no less. And the more intimate they grew, the more distressing it became that his body was made of wood. Every time she touched him, he longed to be able to touch *her* with such grace. Every time they danced, her marvelous fluidity made him feel the weight and brittleness of his own limbs. And when they made love and he entered her with his perpetually hard penis, her ecstasy seemed at an infinite distance from him: a reality of which he was the poor cause and shadow.

His body had to become human. There was no question about it. He didn't know how it would happen, what magic syllable he would unwittingly pronounce, or whose blessing he would all at once undeservedly obtain. But, as if it were a sought-for word on the tip of his tongue, he could almost feel the change, the wood being made flesh. And he could, almost, see the wonder in her eyes.

ST. INEPTUS

Born in third-century Illyria, he soon established a reputation for spilling his food, bruising himself, and tripping over non-existent objects in the street. His parents wanted him to become a doctor, in the hope that the rigorous training would make him more attentive. But he refused. Instead, he spent his time looking for angels in the dark alleyways of his native town, and feeding the stray cats. Even his martyrdom was botched. He felt so terrified, as the wild beasts approached him in the amphitheater, that he forgot the words of the Lord's Prayer.

He has become the patron saint of the clumsy, the tactless, and the unqualified. They are instructed to leave a candle burning for him once a month (making sure that there is nothing flammable in the vicinity). His intercession is said to do more good than harm.

He stands before the council of the gods, invulnerable in his milk-white skin and shining face, as beautiful as Jesus. He loves all things great and small, and all the gods love him.

Except Loki.

Hmmm.

If there is such an event as a divine tragedy, such a being as a perfect victim, why is it that part of us is not displeased when Loki sidles up to the blind Höthr and hands him a javelin cut from the mistletoe, youngest of the bushes? Why do we feel an obscure sense of compensation when the shaft strikes home and all the gods look on in horror? Why do we walk under the green sprig at Christmastide expecting not betrayal, but a kiss?

SPINOZA

To Elizabeth Vitale

For the small boy lying in bed
in the summer shadows, his mind
stretching all the way to the edge
of the universe (which never arrives)
and the end of time (but *then* what?),
knowledge begins in pure awe
and a slowing of the breath
toward sleep, in gradual surrender
to everything that is of the night.

Even before you learned how
to think, you would stand for hours
in the scent of your father's world,
turning the pages, wondering
at the rows of dark spines, perhaps
humming to yourself a *canção*
you had overheard long before.
Sometimes he held you on his lap
and you watched the thick, white-haired finger
move slowly, from right to left.
Aleph: a bull with two prongs
and a dog's snout. *Bet*: a round tongue
in a square mouth. *Gimel*: a chair.
And the vowels floating below
the surface, like sleepy fish.
Not by those words but by
a resonance in your mind
did you know the essential lessons:
that the edge of doubt can be used
to cut through everything that has

hardened into belief;
that the only faith you could trust
was in your own clear awareness.

It is spring now, across the ocean.
Three centuries have gone by
since the rabbis' anathema drove you
from Amsterdam's brick-lined streets.
You were twenty-eight: a small man
with the olive skin and thick eyebrows
of a Portuguese Jew; courteous
to all, good-natured, noble
(if nobility means a passionate
disinterestedness). You liked
a pipe now and then, and felt
neither pity nor undue surprise
at the limitless varieties
of self-imposed human bondage
known as the habitable world.
Exquisitely frugal, like the snake
that forms a circle by holding
its tail in its mouth, you saved
your insight so that there would be
enough for a million days.
I see you in the early '70s
among the Dutch hippies spaced out
on legal hash, the bored women
in garter belts and high heels
on display in the windows, ghosts
of the old Jews Rembrandt
loved to paint, and the small
lively ghost of Anne Frank.
You are inside your shop, still making
lenses for the mind of Europe.
There is not much room. I sit down

on a wooden bench. You offer me
a glass of applejuice. You say,
leaning on the counter, "Rest easy.
All of them have their place
inside eternity. They are
perfect—that is to say, real:
a conclusion not easy to realize.
But all things excellent
are as difficult as they are rare."

THE MYTH OF SISYPHUS

We tend to think of Sisyphus as a tragic hero, condemned by the gods to shoulder his rock sweatily up the mountain, and again up the mountain, forever.

The truth is that Sisyphus is in love with the rock. He cherishes every roughness and every ounce of it. He talks to it, sings to it. It has become the mysterious Other. He even dreams of it as he sleepwalks upward. Life is unimaginable without it, looming always above him like a huge gray moon.

He doesn't realize that at any moment he is permitted to step aside, let the rock hurtle to the bottom, and go home.

Tragedy is the inertial force of the mind.

EVOLUTION

First came eohippus, the dawn horse, dog-sized and equable, barely a meal for the cave bear or the saber-toothed tiger. But different from the others: self-selected, among the rodents, for a swifter destiny. Its toenails had begun to itch. Already it was dreaming of the wind.

Over the ages it found its limbs growing stronger, its snout lengthening. It learned how to whinny. It saw itself turn into the wild ass, the donkey, the horse, the extravagant zebra, and entered history with new molars, an imagination, reins.

In the meantime, two divergent branches had appeared. One, adapting to the rhythm of the waves, curled its tail, shrank, and became the sea horse. The other grew wings. Known as the pegasus, it occasionally gives free rides to deserving poets.

ZEN MASTER

Three feet tall, he sits cross-legged inside a wooden frame in a corner of the living room. He isn't aware of me as I tiptoe closer. Shhh. Leaning over the page, intensely seeing, he rests his left arm on one black-robed knee and lets the small black ritual bib dangle from his neck. So much love in this white porcelain face with its network of glaze-cracks, so much suffering digested and transformed into wisdom. His ink-stained porcelain hands, like two small sea-animals, seem to have eyes at the end of each finger. He has just finished drawing a circle, letting the dark ink thin out as his brush moves around the rice paper, until at the end (the beginning) there is only a faintly brushed trace of it, the mark of a mind running on empty. As for the circle's meaning: Unity? Completion? Nirvana? Give me a break.

He looks down at his handiwork, as I look down at him, satisfied and on the brink of amusement. The mouth doesn't show even the trace of a smile. But the smile is there, somewhere, shining in the heaven of his face like a new moon.

A METAPHOR LEFT OUT IN THE COLD

Coleridge says that human beings are divided into Platonists and Aristotelians. Thinking again about the patience of Job and his later, magnificent rage, I found myself searching for an image. When they search for images, human beings are divided into high Platonists and low Platonists.

One day I read, in a book by an Italian gentleman-farmer, that there is a striking difference between the way lambs and pigs let themselves be slaughtered. The pig, he said, aware and terrified, puts up such a fierce resistance that sometimes five strong men are needed to hold it down. The lamb, though, looks up and meekly allows its throat to be cut, perhaps uttering a soft baa as it goes gentle into that good night.

Ah.

Later, in the interest of accuracy, I spoke with a man who worked in a slaughterhouse. He informed me that, in fact, lambs sense the approaching danger and do struggle to escape. I hung up the phone with a mixture of admiration and regret.

So I couldn't use the image. Not because it wasn't appropriate, but because it wasn't true.

O Pig of God, that takest away the sins of the world!

CASSANDRA

Nobody can stand her anymore. She has become obsessed, boring. Her friends turn the other way. Even her husband no longer listens, as he used to do out of kindness, with glazed eyes.

So she has taken to selling herself on streetcorners. She is attractive enough; the men buy. Up in a cheap hotel room, in the dark, she writhes with them, whispering *nuclear holocaust, acid rain*.

MEISTER ECKHART

God, for the love of God,
is not God. There is nowhere
beyond this Now, this abode
of poverty, birdsong, cut grass,
pure sky above the rooftops,
balanced on the tip of a pin.

How singular! I am nothing.
I am. I will never die.

PALM READING

Slowly, not tentatively, the lines move out from their center light-years away and deeper than the blood that suffuses your hand with a pale pink-yellow radiance. They come, they cross, they dig in, or abruptly break, tracing one small pattern from the network of forgotten lives. All of it becomes clear in the clarity of vision. What was blurred, unintelligible, sharpens to perfect simplicity: the sound of rain on the toyroom window; fragments of a Japanese vase left lying beneath the altar.

    Where was the first mistake,
the groove
in the heart, repeated
so often that it turned into
truth? The eye
sees eye,
the hand grasps nothing
but hand, the moon rises
out of deepest flesh
and the whole body
is illumined
in its night.

A LONG ENGAGEMENT

She was a Leo, he (although he despised astrology) was a Unicorn. The combination is notoriously difficult. They did everything they could to avoid it, and when that was no longer possible, they took every precaution. She sheathed her claws. He couldn't hide his horn.

Difficult, but more fruitful than they could have imagined. Over the course of many years, they learned to fight bloodlessly. He vividly remembered the moment when he was first able to hear the terror of her roar without galloping away. After that, their fights became bearable, even exhilarating. They learned to live with two paws (hoofs) in each other's world, and to cook separately. Having finished his grass salad (he was always done first), he would spend the rest of the meal looking at her, sharing her pleasure as she gnawed on a bleeding, almost-raw slab of mutton or beef.

In the evening they would lie down together as peaceably as in Isaiah's garden.

PAUL OF TARSUS

Stepping from the clear air of the gospel
into your mind,
I found myself hemmed in, darkened,
struggling for my natural breath.
Yes, Brother, I know
what you glimpsed on the road to Damascus:
the sense of boundless freedom
that shot, electric, through every
nerve in your body, and all
the strictures of Thou Shalt Not
gave way, the dead weight of authority
lifted, and your only duty
was to the law
written in your inmost heart.
You were born again. But with
the bloody remains of your former
self smeared over you; ardent
and headstrong as usual, you leapt
from the delivery room table
straight out into the world
to teach the Gentiles your truth.
You left no time for yourself
to remain a child, to grow
inside the kingdom of heaven
slowly and naturally
as a tree grows by the water streams,
then ripens and bears fruit
in its own season; no time
for your dogmatism and intolerance and resentment
to fall away by themselves,
letting you shed your guilt
as your old enemy the serpent
sheds his skin. And so

you remained with a past, a future,
and a now caught between them, in which
God-the-Judge kept watching you
through a one-way mirror, darkly.

I would like to arrange a meeting
between you and the true messiah
(you can call him Jesus if you like).
I would have you sit in my back yard
on a perfect day like today,
with a continuo of birdsong
and a mild breeze stirring the fig tree,
a fresh-baked sourdough
baguette on the picnic table,
three glasses, and a bottle
of a nice California port.
He might not say a word
of the Good News according to summer.
Perhaps it would be enough
to see him, face to face,
as he sips the wine and hands you
a piece of the bread: take;
eat; this is your body.

CERBERUS

His three fierce mastiff-heads bloodcurdlingly bark. No spirit may enter the Elysian Fields until he is satisfied that it is truly at peace. Some have tried to bribe him, but he is incorruptible. Some have tried to sneak past, but he tore the memory of their bodies to agonized shreds. Pain outlasts its vehicle.

Even he, though, was a puppy once. He sometimes looks out at the vast crowd milling desperately by the gates of horn (or is it the gates of ivory?—he can never keep his classical references straight), and feels a twinge of pity for them, like a minor third. How impatient they are. How they would love to be able to pat him on each of his heads, say "Nice doggy," and move on. But they are no longer living in the trivial, safe universe of their desires. Everything here is real.

COURTESY

No, it is not a matter of bows and fine speeches. We've had enough of that.

It is (how best to phrase it?) a natural ease, a politeness of the heart, the kind of step backward the God of the cabalists once took, so that the universe of the other can exist. And I, who am a slow student of the art, find it where I can, in Montaigne and Spinoza, the smile of a Benedictine nun through a latticed parlor, an old Hasid in Jerusalem giving a coin to a beggar and saying "Thank-you" for the opportunity of fulfilling a commandment. I have seen it among the poor, who, like the serpent in Eden, learn humility by staying on the ground. And among the great, those noblemen and ladies in Shakespeare moving with such grace through their disasters: the duke in the forest of Arden, Hermione answering the maddened king, Brutus before the last battle, taking the lute from under the arm of his sleeping boy-servant, gently.

ABRAHAM

What had become very clear to him that night on the fast-disappearing summer pavements—the air thick with jasmine, the bony cats sniffing among the garbage heaps—was that he would be able to take along: nothing. Precisely nothing. Not even the memory of his face, glimpsed some morning in the bathroom mirror, or the name of the woman he had loved. He would have to leave it all behind, here, in this world, which had come to fit him like his own skin. Soon enough, in due time, perhaps in no time at all, he would have to step out beyond the boundaries of his life, move where there is no place to move, grope in the blinding light, toward a goal he could be sure of never reaching.

THE PARABLE OF THE SOWER

A sower went forth to sow. Some of his seeds fell upon stony places. Centuries passed; millennia. And the seeds remained. And the stones crumbled and became good soil, and the seeds brought forth fruit.

"Wait a minute," said one listener. "You can't play fast and loose that way with the natural facts. The seeds would die long before the soil could receive them."

"Why would they die?"

"Because they can't hold out in stony places, for thousands of years."

"But, my dear, what kind of seeds do you think we're talking about?"

FRANCIS

Blessed are the poor in spirit,
who realize that they have no more
than what is their own. They stand
tiptoe in the bright kingdom
of the moment, like children looking
down from the bedroom window,
waving hello, goodbye.

FOUR WATERCOLORS BY TAO-CHI

Bamboo

Sometimes I have spent hours face to face with a single stalk, watching for its essence, listening, waiting on the sheer edge of attention, until my arm begins to sway in the light wind, and my brush is blown across the page, along the branches, out to the tendrils and leaves, the last spray turns into calligraphy, moves down the lines of verse, and with one final, half-dry flourish: signs my name.

Lakeside Geese

Desolation. The forest's bones. Blunt strokes of gray and black, ink-spots sprayed over rocks, among twigs jutting out from the thick snow. Black clouds over sky and ground, through which, high up, geese

plunge.

Off to the side a man, transparent, with a short travel-staff, stands halfway across the frail wooden bridge.

When it is cold, you die of cold.

Orchid and Rock

I have painted them in the same mild tones of grayish green.

The orchid supports itself on its thin stem, under the arch of a long, grasslike leaf. The rock, moss-speckled, is suspended in air, yet it keeps its composure. Each may represent whatever you wish, though I have painted them from life, which has no symbols.

When speech comes from a quiet heart, it has the strength of the orchid, and the fragrance of rock.

Wilderness Cottage

They say that I honor tradition, that I'm a worthy disciple. But I am simply myself. The beards and eyebrows of the ancestors can't grow on my face, nor can their bowels function in my belly. If my paintings occasionally look like some ancient master's, he's the one who is following me, not vice versa. When have I ever studied the great ones without turning them upside down?

The truth is that mountains, rivers, peach blossoms, artichokes have requested me to speak for them. They find a language through me; I find a language through them. When the spirit of Nature joins with my spirit, both are transformed. So that, in the end, everything leads back to me.

MATHEMATICS

Any place you look is an entrance. The equals-sign. That fabulous Arab invention, zero. The square root of minus one.

But then, *all* numbers are imaginary from the start. (When did I last meet a 7?) This is childishness, or pure art, where the more beautiful a solution is, the truer. Don't worry, the technicians will find a use for it. Let x stand for you.

SINAI

Everyone knows what happened at the bottom of Mount Sinai, but no one mentions what happened on the top. In a way, this is unavoidable: the eye can't see itself, the equation can't prove itself. Nevertheless, a few of our sages have spoken. (In order to say anything, they had to be there.)

Rabbi Levi said, "On the top of Mount Sinai, Moses was given the choice of receiving the commandments or seeing God face to face. He knew that he could not see God without first dying. It was like looking into a mirror with no reflection inside."

Rabbi Ezra said, "Moses did receive a commandment, but only one, only the First. All the others blended into silence, as all colors blend into white."

Rabbi Gamaliel said, "Moses received only the first phrase of the First Commandment: I am the Unnamable."

Rabbi Elhanan said, "Moses saw on Sinai what he had heard from the Burning Bush. There was just one message: I am."

Rabbi Samuel said, "Not even that. The only word the Unnamable whispered was *I*."

Rabbi Yosi said, "In the holy tongue, *I* is *anokhi: aleph-nun-kaph-yod*. What Moses received from God was the first letter of *I*."

But *aleph* is a silent letter.

Rabbi Yosi said, "Just so."

NARCISSUS

It was not the image of his own face that transfixed him as he bent down over the pool. He had seen that face often before: in mirrors, in a thousand photographs, in women's eyes. It was an undistinguished face, but handsome enough, with its long eyelashes, full lips, and stately nose sloping to a curious plateau near the tip.

No, it was something else now that rooted him to the spot. Kneeling there, gazing into the so taken-for-granted form, he grew more and more poignantly aware that it was mere surface. When the water was calm, *it* was calm; when the water rippled at the touch of a leaf or a fish, it too rippled; or broke apart when he churned the water with his hand. More and more fascinated, he kept staring through the image of his face into the depths beneath, filled with a multitude of other, moving, shadowy forms. He knew that if he stayed there long and patiently enough, he would be able to see straight through to the bottom. And at that moment, he knew, the image would disappear.

PICASSO

1

A large man with the head of a bull
sits on the right side of the etching.
He is draped in white linen; his powerful
chest is bare; on his left thigh
a colossal penis begins
to stir. He gazes with longing
and incomprehension at the naked
woman in the left foreground,
who is lying on a couch. Her breasts
look succulent, the curve of her hips
an invitation to a voyage
beyond the senses. She is full-face,
staring out at us, brazenly,
with no desire, and in total
awareness of her sexual power.
The minotaur's hairy left hand
absentmindedly grips a wine glass.
He feels drunk with her nakedness, her beauty.
If he can't find a way, soon,
of expressing how much he hates her,
there is no telling what he'll do.

2

The figure of a youth. Lovely,
an Apollo with large, sad eyes.
In his hair twines a wreath of laurel.
Another wreath twines around
the bust he has made, which sits
on a column, as tall as he is.
He is resting his hand, the one
with the sculpting-knife, on the edge.
The bust is in profile, almost

double life-size, inhuman,
serene, with a high-arched nose
and an unpupiled eye set far back
in its face. It is turned
toward the sad-eyed young sculptor.
Its marble lips, slightly parted, seem
to be telling him something.

AT THE ZOO

Orangutans

Such big sweet ugly faces. There are many visitors, so the youngest, leaning over, has lifted his rump straight up into the air. The two large ones are over by the pool, with burlap bags over their heads and around their shoulders, like rabbis. We stand and watch them on their simulated mountain. Is it time to take out our sandwiches? Then one unwraps himself (peek-a-boo) and sticks his thumb in his mouth.

Pygmy Hippo

Mud! What a comfort on a hot day. His oily, eggplant-purple skin is sunk in it up to his head. We look on in appreciation of such self-assured indolence. His ears flick, like tiny propellers.

Elephants

Homage to you, old wrinkled Buddhas. One of them is using her trunk now to sweep the remnants of hay from lunch into a neat pile. The other turns around and ambles off at a graceful, meditative pace, then stops: and out plop two huge turds. All the children crinkle their noses in disgust. "Eeeuuw!"

Feeding-time at the Lion House

Some of them are roaring in unison at the cage doors. Some pace back and forth, or stand licking their chops.

Two o'clock arrives, and the keepers with wheelbarrows of beef.

So. It has come to this.

"Under your mother's pillow," he said. "That's where the key is. Unlock my cage and your golden ball is yours. Otherwise, no deal."

He was certainly a tough-looking character. Nine feet tall, with a linebacker's physique and a shaggy, chest-length beard (a few strands of wet pond-moss peeped out from among the black hairs). He was glaring at me most ferociously. I glared right back. I knew I would have to enter the royal bedroom with my right hand on my dagger, ready for blood. But there was no way I was going to give up that golden ball.

Both of us meant business.

Pluto sits on his ebony throne enchanted. "Beautiful," he sighs. "Ah, beautiful." Iron tears trickle down his cheeks. He puts his hand on Persephone's arm. "My dear," he says, "we must grant this young man's request."

The young queen thinks for a moment. She has ripened since her first, unwilling, visit to the underworld, when all the forms were shadowy, and behind each shadow lurked a fear. Now she can see clearly in the dreamlight. She is on a first-name basis with all the inhabitants, from the gentlest to the most savage. She has learned never to look back.

But this poor boy, this exquisite singer, will have a hard time ahead of him; she can tell by looking at his eyes. It is one thing to charm animals, trees, and rocks, and quite another to be in harmony with a woman. She recognizes his attitude, she has seen it before: fear protected by longing. Hence the bridal image, forever unattainable, forever ideal. No wonder Eurydice took the serpent's way out. Girls who are seen that way grow up to be maenads. If only, she thinks: if only there were some way to tell him. But, of course, he will have to learn for himself. To lose his love again and again, precipitously, as if by chance. To be torn in pieces, again and again.

She turns to the king. "Yes, darling," she says. "Let them go."

He had tried everything: new batteries, new bulb, a new off-and-on switch.

Useless.

Nada.

Not even a flicker.

It was uncomfortable wearing defective merchandise. He would have loved to file it away in some drawer and forget about it. But that too was impossible. It had apparently been installed as a permanent feature of his physiognomy. There it remained, an inescapable memorandum, six inches above his head and slightly tilted to one side, at the rakish angle at which a gentleman might wear a boater.

YESHU OF NAZARETH

1

You came to me when I was nine,
with the sheen that forbidden joys have.

When I asked about you, the rabbi's
face clamped into a cold
smile. Just behind his words
I could sense the fear and repugnance;
something was wrong; I had bungled
into a high-security
area, like sex. No clearance.
You were the noisy skeleton
in our closet, the pile of dust
swept under our soul's rug, the prodigal
son who had stayed abroad
and grown rich and famous selling
bacon. How could I not tiptoe
out of my fathers' house
to meet you on every high mountain
and under every green tree?

2

Much later, the message became clear:
"What I have undergone
to reach the kingdom inside us,
you must undergo too,
and it will be no easier
for you, though I have gone first."

3

Golgotha. Were you unable
to endure one moment longer
the body's agony, the failure,

74

the impossible desolation
by what you most trusted? And yet
this too had to be lived.
There was no outside heaven
waiting for you. Despair
had to be made your own
since you had, somewhere, willed it,
and yourself had given yourself
that cup
to drink, to the bitter last drop.
You walked into perfect horror
open-eyed, leaving behind
everything. As if you were walking
into the final room
of your own house.

These fellows with the third-chakra problems, who think they have arrived. "I am the avatar." "I have the truth." It is like advertising Up with a sign for Down. *Develop a mind*, the Diamond Sutra says, *that alights nowhere*.

I myself take Chao-chou Ts'ung-shen as an exemplar. He attained enlightenment (ha!) in 795, at the age of seventeen, stayed put for the next forty years until his Zen Master died, then went out on a twenty-year pilgrimage to hone his insight. Only when he was eighty years old did he feel ready to teach. He died at the age of 120. His eloquence was so profound and subtle, legend says, that light seemed to play about his lips as he spoke.

One day Chao-chou said to the assembly, "Even the *word* 'Buddha' makes me want to throw up."

A monk bowed and asked, "Then how do you teach people?"

Chao-chou said, "Buddha! Buddha!"

A RELUCTANT BODHISATTVA

Seven or eight years before, she had been awakened in the middle of the night by two lines of silvery energy undulating up either side of her spine like snakes. She found herself observing the strange sensation, detached but curious. When the energy reached the top of her head, it turned into a nuclear explosion, blasting her out into a dimension of pure bliss. There was nothing there—or nothing but light—if you could call it light. Later, her husband told her that her body, whether in joy or relief, had spent those hours continuously sobbing. Keeping watch, he had felt like one of the guardian demons before the gates of a Japanese temple.

It was not that she was ungrateful for the energy. True, she had rebelled against it for months, feeling that it was a rude, uninvited guest, or an accidental fetus that she would gladly have aborted if she could. But little by little she came to trust it, then to love it, and to be in awe of its fierce intelligence, which kept compelling her to let go of her fears and smallnesses, obstacles in the path of its current. Yes, she realized it was a long process; she knew that when she could finally accept the gift with all her heart, she herself would become gift, to everyone who could receive her. But in the often agonizing stages of letting go, she would long to be in another body, unvisited by spiritual grace, unspecial, ordinary. She imagined herself as a simple housewife, cooking, cleaning, enjoying a barbecue now and then with a small circle of friends, gliding upon the smooth surface of things like a skater. Sometimes she would stare for a long time at some object in the kitchen—a coffee mug, a straw place mat, an apple—and weep with envy. *Apple. Mug.* How simple it was for them, blessed with a name and form, complete, never having to learn to surrender.

THE GIFT

Besides the small gifts that he delighted in giving her when the chance came along—the dinners out, the poems, Palestrina, the single red rose every few weeks, the anniversary ring, simple as her wedding ring but crowned with a rainbow opal—he wanted to give her something of supreme value.

There were two posters in their bedroom. On the wall opposite the bed, a large color photograph of Maitreya, the future Buddha: long, elegant wooden fingers almost touching his cheek, head slightly tilted to the right, on his serene face a small, heartwarming smile, as if he was enjoying the most delicious of private jokes.

This mind he knew inside and out. He didn't need to embody it.

But on the wall above the bed, there was another photo: one of the erotic temple sculptures from Khajuraho. He always thought of the male figure in it as Rama, the marriage god, the god of the happy ending, who has found and reclaimed his Sita among the demons, in the land of the dead. Now they stand reunited in each other's arms. She has her back toward the viewer. Naked except for a braided belt, she clasps Rama around the neck in a surrender so complete that it makes her whole body weightless. Rama, meanwhile, all creation bursting inside his veins, feels his body as if for the first time, more vigorous, more male than he could ever have imagined. His penis rests on her right thigh, stretching, as if it has awakened from a long sleep.

He knew, of course, that the gift was not his to give. It was beyond his conscious will; there was no way he could touch it, much less hand it to her. But when he lay beside her, at their quietest moments, he could see it in her eyes, reflected as in a medium of supreme clarity and love.

THE SENSE OF PROPORTION

There are at least one hundred billion galaxies in the universe. Each galaxy contains at least one hundred billion stars. Each star illuminates an uncounted number of planets, each of which may support inconceivable forms of life.

From most points of view, the green earth is smaller than an electron.

All this is happening within your mind.

MONTAIGNE

The beginning of wisdom is to know
that we don't know. How sweet it is.
To retire from the object and spend
one's long, leisure-filled days
curiously puttering around
the subject. Your patron saint,
the Greek with the frog's face, taught it:
honesty, the primary point
and supreme pleasure: to drift
in the ever-strange stream of the mind
hunched on a lily pad, watching.

What virtue is more attractive
than candor? Who isn't charmed
by the most trivial detail
of a life told just as it happens,
no apologies, no pretense,
and a child-bright fascination
with the mystery of the self,
that that which (as it were) is—
eternal
limitless
empty
—locks itself
in a cell, in
two cells, four, a million,
to be molded by time and space
into another kind of
identity: supple, tentative,
compassionate, loud-voiced, a bald
half-Jewish Frenchman who at first
liked radishes; then didn't; then wound up
liking them after all.

PENELOPE

He had heard from her several times during his long absence. Three letters managed to arrive at Troy, one at Calypso's island, and one at the cave of Polyphemus (it was delivered by a sheep). All of them written on the same light-blue 5 × 8″ stationery, in her girlish, touchingly fluid handwriting, with looped *thetas*, and *nus* as round as *upsilons*. "Things are difficult but all is well. . . . How ripe I have become for you. . . . Much love . . . " The longer he was away, the more intensely he felt the gravitation of that love. Even on Aeaea or Ogygia, caught up in the embrace of one of the importunate, multi-orgasmic nymphs whom it was his fate to satisfy, he could sense her presence, could see her in bed or walking on the beach or sitting at her loom, as faithful to him, body and heart, as he was to her in his heart alone, alas.

Now, for the first time in twenty years, he stands before her. The suitors have gone home, disappointed but polite. The whole household—servants, maids, swine, cattle, chickens, and the astonished dogs—have retired. There are just the two of them. She looks, at fifty-three, even more beautiful, more transparent, than when he last saw her: her radiance like a flame that has outgrown its need for fuel. He is so proud of who she has become.

The silence deepens.

He stands there for a long time before letting himself plunge to the bottom of her eyes.

"Ooh, make it a sad story," the children said. "Make it a sad, sad story." They were sitting on the fence in the late February sunlight. They had all been changed into birds.

"Once there was a needle," I began, "and every time it pierced the lips . . . "

"Oh," cried the children, "we know about *that* kind of sorrow. Tell us about the other."

I must admit that I was reluctant to continue. The sunlight in the yard was so poignant after a day of rain. I could hear their little claws skittering along the fence.

"All right," I said. "Once there was a needle, and every time it pierced the eyes . . . "

VERMEER

Quia respexit humilitatem
ancillae suae. LUKE 1:48

She stands by the table, poised
at the center of your vision,
with her left hand
just barely on
the pitcher's handle, and her right
lightly touching the windowframe.
Serene as a clear sky, luminous
in her blue dress and many-toned
white cotton wimple, she is looking
nowhere. Upon her lips
is the subtlest and most lovely
of smiles, caught
for an instant
like a snowflake in a warm hand.
How weightless her body feels
as she stands, absorbed, within this
fulfillment that has brought more
than any harbinger could.
She looks down with an infinite
tenderness in her eyes,
as though the light at the window
were a newborn child
and her arms open enough
to hold it on her breast, forever.

NOTES

MANJUSHRI

A wooden statue, formerly on the altar of the Maui Zendo.

The last sentence is adapted from a short dialogue in Robert Aitken's "Selections from Coyote Roshi Goroku," *Coyote's Journal*, Wingbow, 1982.

JEROME

"Dürer's engraving": *St. Jerome*, 1514.

THE ANNUNCIATION

I have taken the idea in the last paragraph from Rilke's early poem "Verkündigung."

TAO-CHI

Bird Watching, watercolor in the Arthur M. Sackler Collection at the Metropolitan Museum of Art, New York. See Marilyn Fu and Wen Fong's excellent *The Wilderness Colors of Tao-chi*, Metropolitan Museum of Art, 1973.

SPINOZA

Several facts in the description of Spinoza are taken from Johannes Colerus's biography (1706).

ZEN MASTER

A doll, modeled after Shunryu Suzuki Roshi, by Cassandra Light.

COURTESY

"Brutus . . . ": This gesture is movingly noticed in Hofmannsthal's essay "Shakespeare's Kings and Noblemen," translated by Tania and James Stern, in Hugo von Hofmannsthal, *Selected Prose*, Pantheon, 1952.

FOUR WATERCOLORS BY TAO-CHI

All four are reproduced in *The Wilderness Colors of Tao-chi*.

Lakeside Geese

A monk asked Tung-shan, "How can one escape from heat and cold?"

The Master said, "Why don't you go to a place where there is neither heat nor cold?"

The monk said, "What kind of place is that?"

The Master said, "When it is hot, you die of heat. When it is cold, you die of cold."

(*The Recorded Dialogues of Ch'an Master Tung-shan Liang-chieh*)

Wilderness Cottage

In this section I have borrowed extensively from Tao-chi's *Notes on Painting*.

PICASSO

1: *Sculptor and Reclining Model by a Window Viewing a Sculptured Head* and *Drinking Minotaur and Reclining Woman.*

2: *Young Sculptor at Work.* The three etchings are reproduced in *Picasso for Vollard*, Harry N. Abrams, Inc., 1956.

THE HALO THAT WOULD NOT LIGHT

The title is from Wallace Stevens's notebook and was first published in George S. Lensing, *Wallace Stevens: A Poet's Growth*, Louisiana State University Press, 1986.

SPIRITUAL TEACHING

"One day . . . ": From *The Recorded Dialogues of Ch'an Master Chao-chou Ts'ung-shen.*

THE GIFT

The sculpture is from the Citragupta Temple, Khajuraho. See Heinrich Zimmer, *The Art of Indian Asia*, Pantheon, 1955, vol. 2, plate 318.

VERMEER

Young Woman With a Water Jug, in the Metropolitan Museum of Art, New York. Reproduced on the cover of this book.

ABOUT THE AUTHOR

Stephen Mitchell was born in Brooklyn, New York, in 1943 and studied at Amherst, the University of Paris, and Yale. His previous books include *Dropping Ashes on the Buddha*, *The Selected Poetry of Rainer Maria Rilke*, *The Book of Job*, *Tao Te Ching*, and *The Enlightened Heart*. He lives with his wife, Vicki Chang, an acupuncturist and healer, in Berkeley, California.